Chugach Range

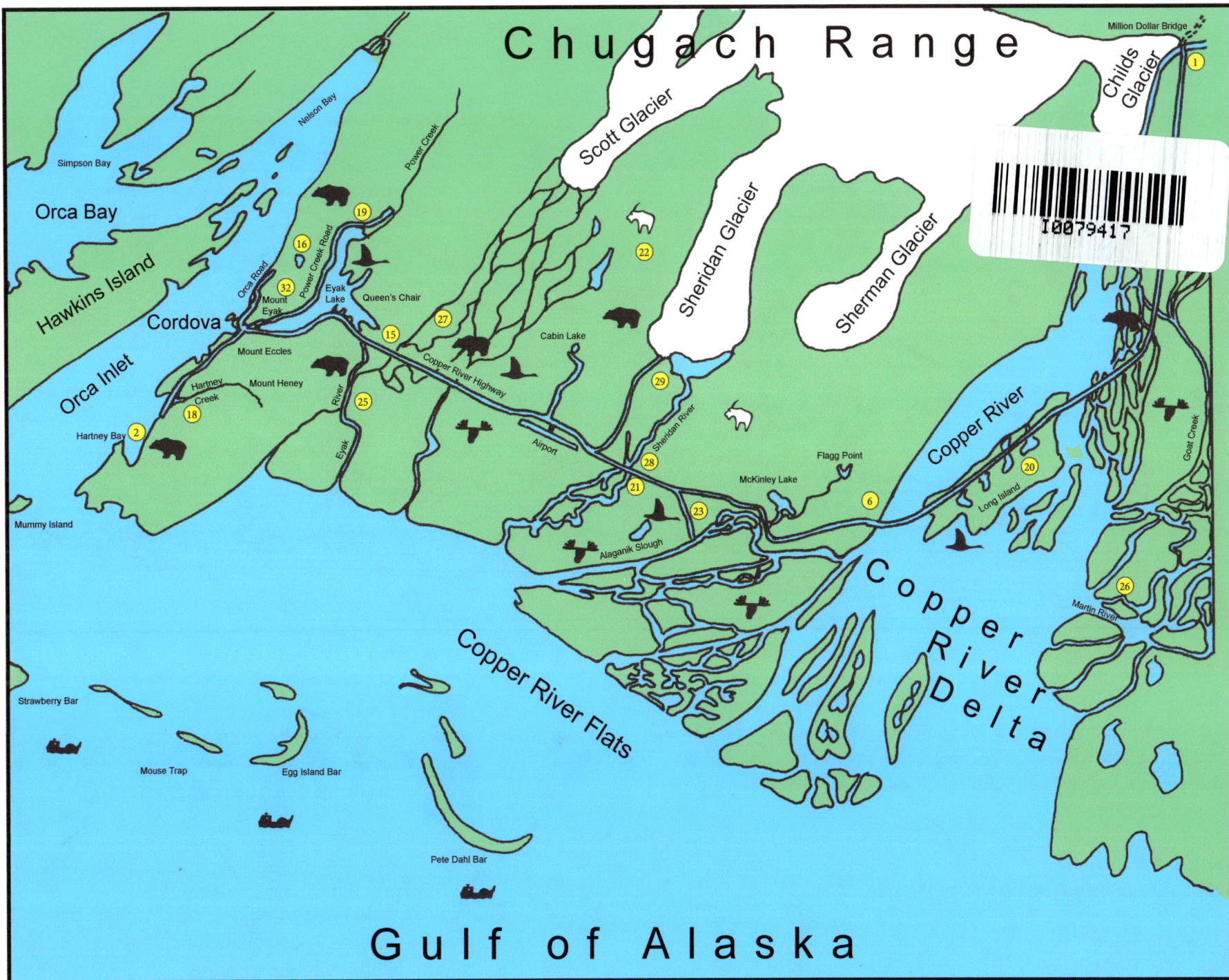

Million Dollar Bridge

Childs Glacier

Scott Glacier

Sheridan Glacier

Sherman Glacier

1

Simpson Bay

Orca Bay

Nelson Bay

Power Creek

Hawkins Island

19

16

Orca Road

Power Creek Road

32

Mount Eyak

Eyak Lake

Queen's Chair

22

27

Cordova

Mount Eccles

15

Copper River Highway

Cabin Lake

29

Orca Inlet

Hartney Creek

Mount Heney

River

25

Eyak

Airport

Sheridan River

Copper River

18

2

Hartney Bay

28

Flagg Point

McKinley Lake

20

Long Island

Mummy Island

21

23

6

Goat Creek

Alaganik Slough

26

Martin River

Strawberry Bar

Copper River Flats

Copper River Delta

Mouse Trap

Egg Island Bar

Pete Dahl Bar

Gulf of Alaska

More than just a coloring book, this is a guide to Cordova activities to help you locate wildlife and to learn a little about the area.

The map on the first page shows wildlife symbols and selected page locations to assist you.

The scenes found in this book depict actual locations as they were in 1986 except for page 2 which was added for this edition.

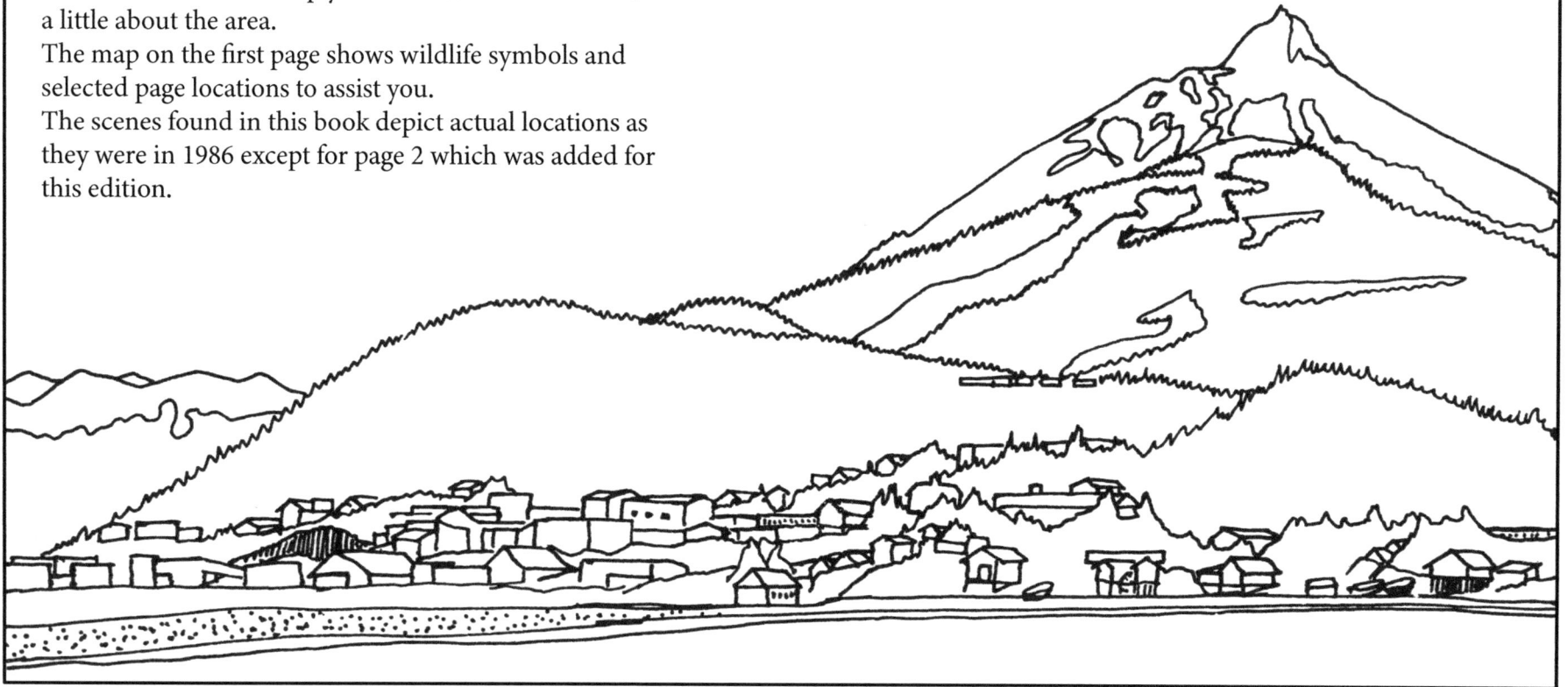

ISBN 0-9607358-5-2
First Printing February 1986

Second Printing December 2024
ISBN 978-1-954896-06-2

Michael C. Anderson
Author and Artist
P.O. Box 1603
Cordova, AK 99574-1603
michaelandersonartist.com

Fathom Publishing Company
PO Box 200448
Anchorage, AK 99520-0448
fathompublishing.com

Coloring Cordova

Doings for a rainy day

The Million Dollar Bridge and Childs Glacier are at Mile 52, Copper River Highway. It is exciting to view bergs calving from Childs Glacier. The bridge was build in 1910 by the Copper River and Northwestern Railroad and was damaged in the 1964 Alaska Earthquake. The fallen section was raised and then the 38 Mile Bridge washed out.

Millions of shorebirds migrate through the Copper River Delta in early May. They feed on tiny intertidal invertebrates to refuel before flying farther north. They are easily seen at Hartney Bay.

Mt. Eccles rises above Cordova with its Dancing Lady and Running Bear. Can you locate their snow and rock shapes on the real mountain? A raven, the creator of the world according to Native legend, watches gulls flying to their bathing area on Lake Eyak.

3

The Harbor Memorial Park is a tribute to the courage of the fishermen. The sculpture, by Cordova's Joan Bugbee Jackson, depicts a fisherman on a rolling deck raising his fist to the storm. The Harbor Memorial Park is one of the city's several parks.

Canneries processing salmon, herring, crab, and halibut dominate the waterfront of this fishing town. This boat makes a delivery of Dungeness crab at a cannery. The crabs are unloaded into a metal box that is hoisted to the dock. Fish pumps are used to unload salmon and herring.

Gillnet boats are tied at Mile 27 of the Copper River Highway just upriver of the fishing area. The boats with the big reel at the front of the boat are called bowpickers. Gillnet fishermen use the reel to pull in their nets while they "pick" salmon that have been caught by the gills.

A salmon seiner uses a 900-foot-long net stretched against the current in a u-shape to catch salmon. The net is then pulled into a circle and pursed closed at the bottom to trap the fish. These fishermen are retrieving the net so that they can brail the fish aboard the boat.

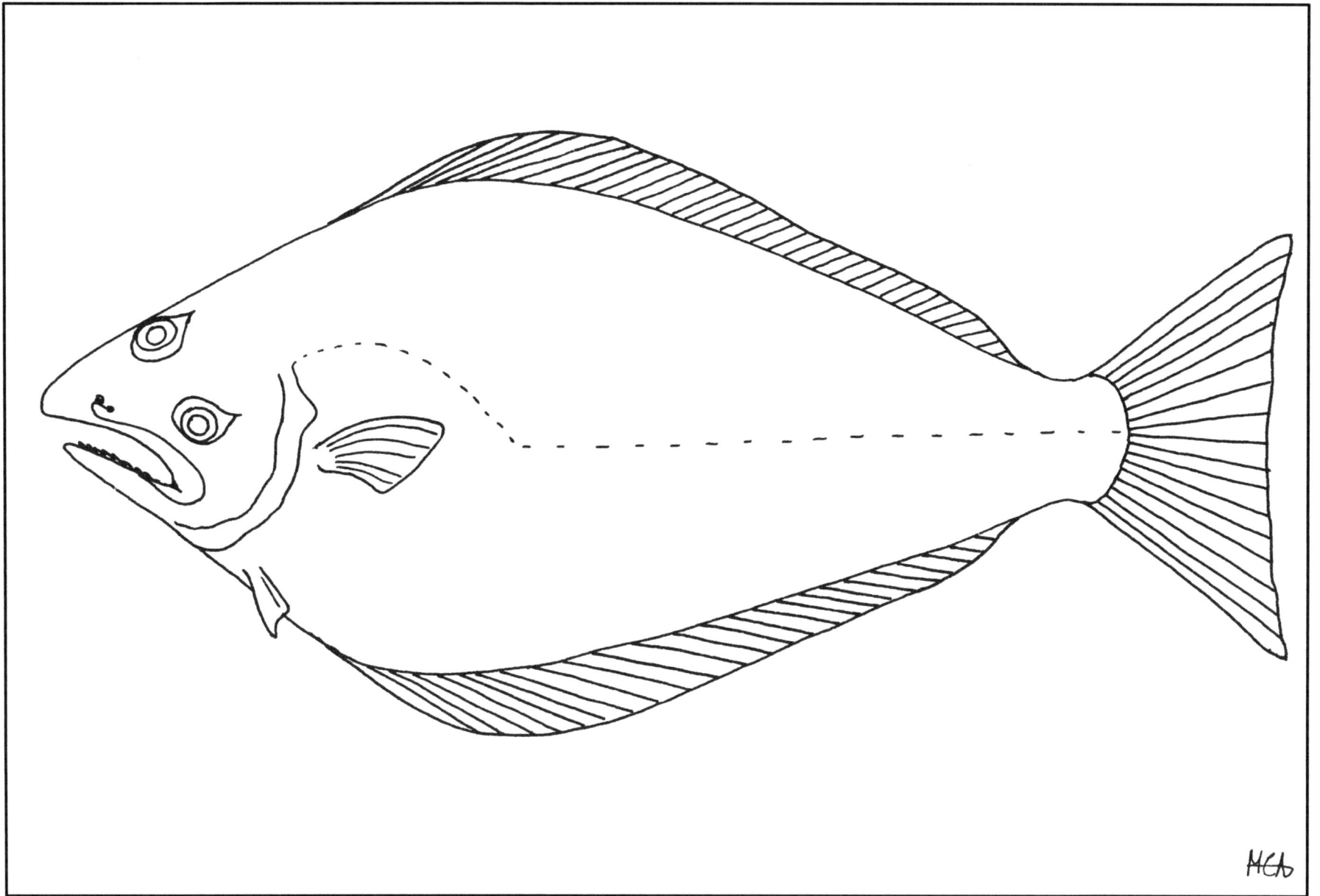

Halibut live flat on the sea floor so they need two eyes on one side looking up. They grow to be huge and can swallow a large crab whole. A heavy line, a stick to wind it around, a weight, and a large hook baited with herring is all the tackle you need to try catching one at the docks.

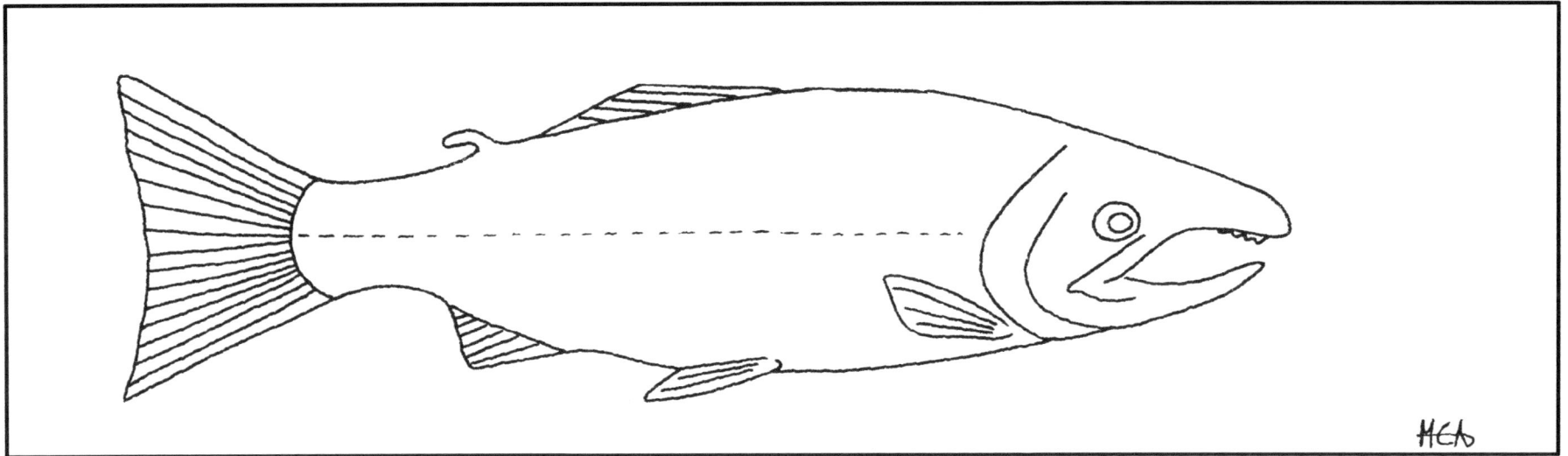

Five kinds of salmon return each summer to Orca Inlet and the rivers of the Copper Delta. Red and King Salmon start returning in May, then Pink and Chum Salmon in mid-summer, followed by Silver Salmon in late summer and fall.

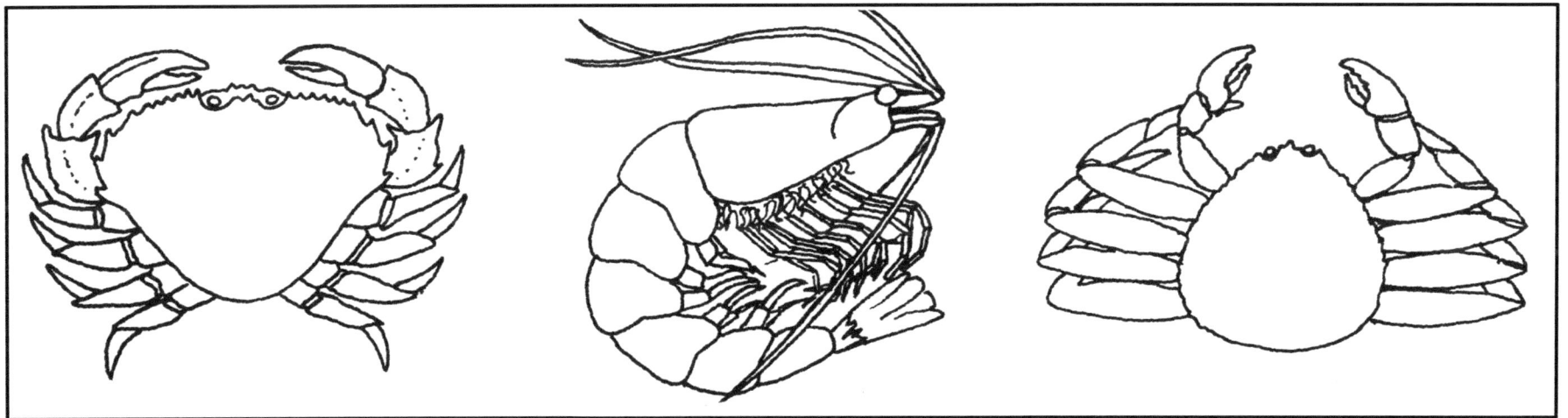

Dungeness and Tanner Crab and Shrimp are harvested during the fall and winter. They are caught in Prince William Sound and in the Gulf of Alaska. Special traps of mesh and steel, called pots shown on the next page, are used to catch these delicious shellfish.

9

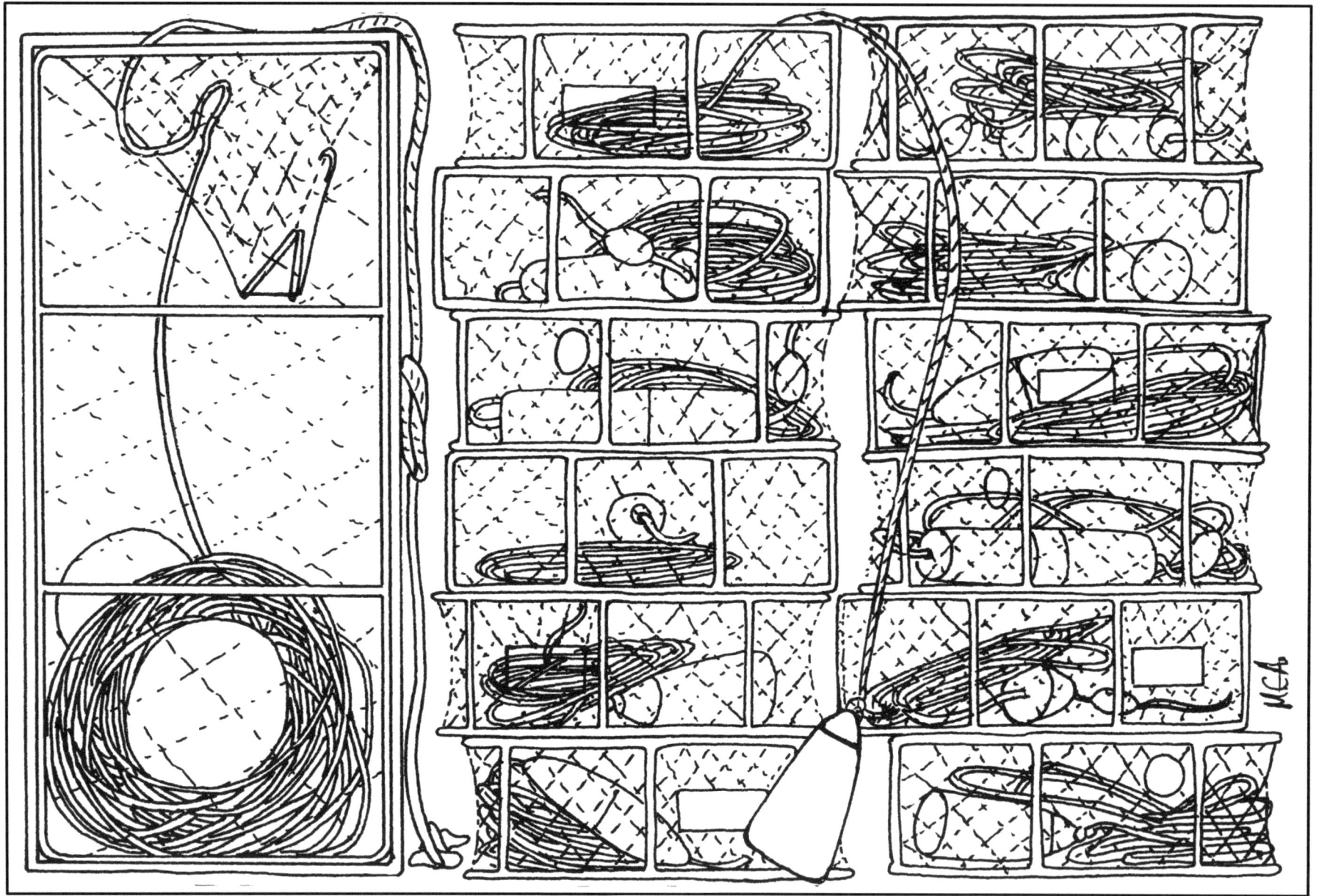

Crab pots are stacked waiting for the crab season. In use, the pots rest on the bottom and are connected to surface marker bouys by long lines. The crab walk in the pot's funnel opening after the bait and can't find their way out of the pot. An escape hole is provided for small crab.

The Alaska Marine Highway ferry is the only way to drive to Cordova. A ride during the day is a great way to see the whales, boats, mountains, and birds of the Sound.

Pods of Orca Whales often escort the ferry and other boats on their travels. You'll see the big dorsal fin and white patches when they surface on the run, called porpoising. The older males average 23 feet in length and have the tallest dorsal fins.

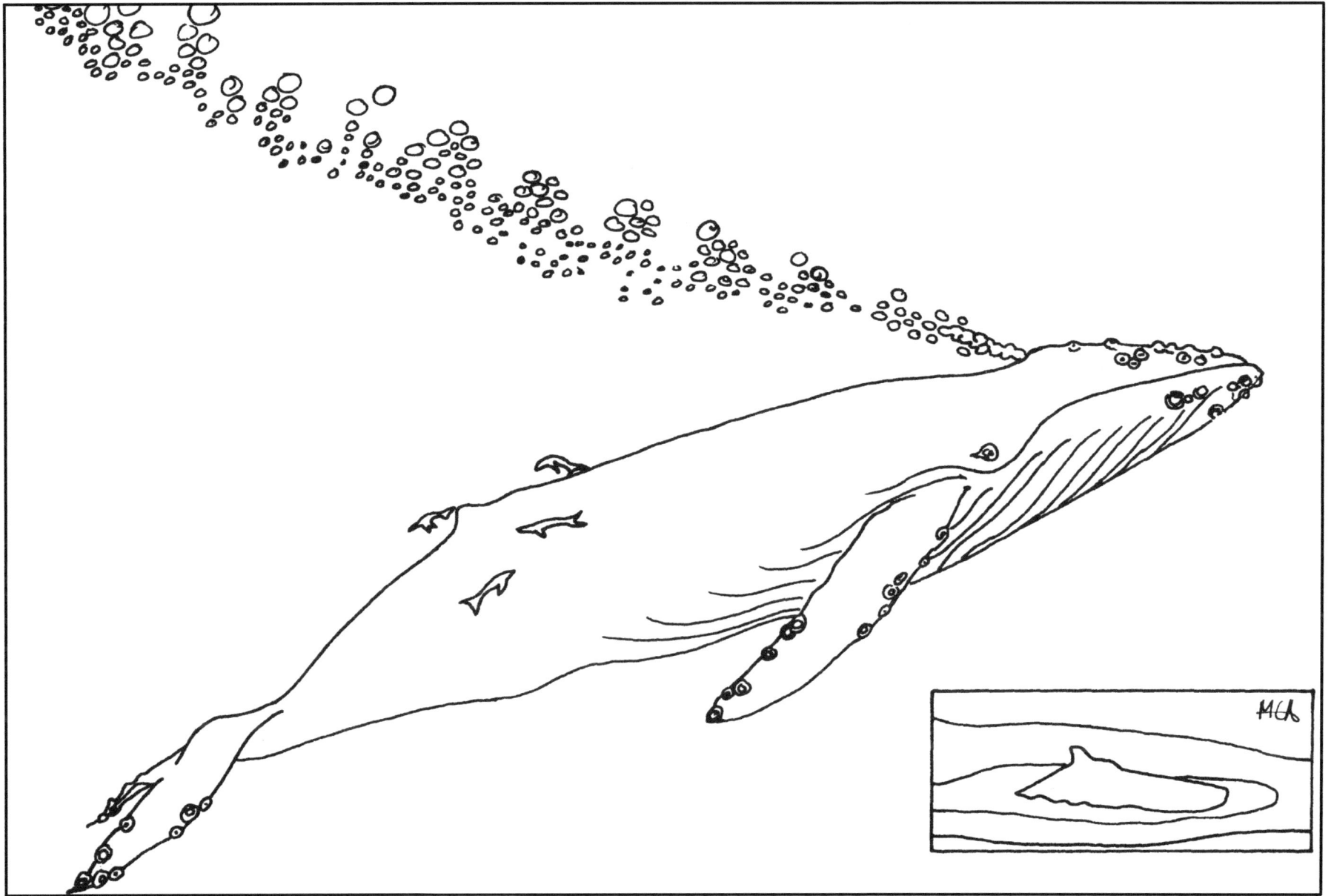

Humpback Whales, though they can grow to 53 feet in length, are harder to see. Usually you'll only see a soft balloon-shaped blow and a small lumpy dorsal fin when the whale takes a breath, like the inset picture. Notice the small fish and barnacles that live with and on this whale.

13

This sea otter floats on his back while eating a crab. They are easy to spot almost anywhere in Orca Inlet, along Orca Road north of town, or even in the small boat harbor. Once hunted near extinction for their fine fur, they have recovered and are now very abundant.

Bald Eagles change guard on their nest north of Mile 7. The eagles' white heads are easily spotted and a careful watcher will see their large nests in the dead tree stands. Please watch from a distance as the eagles will be disturbed if you get near to their nest.

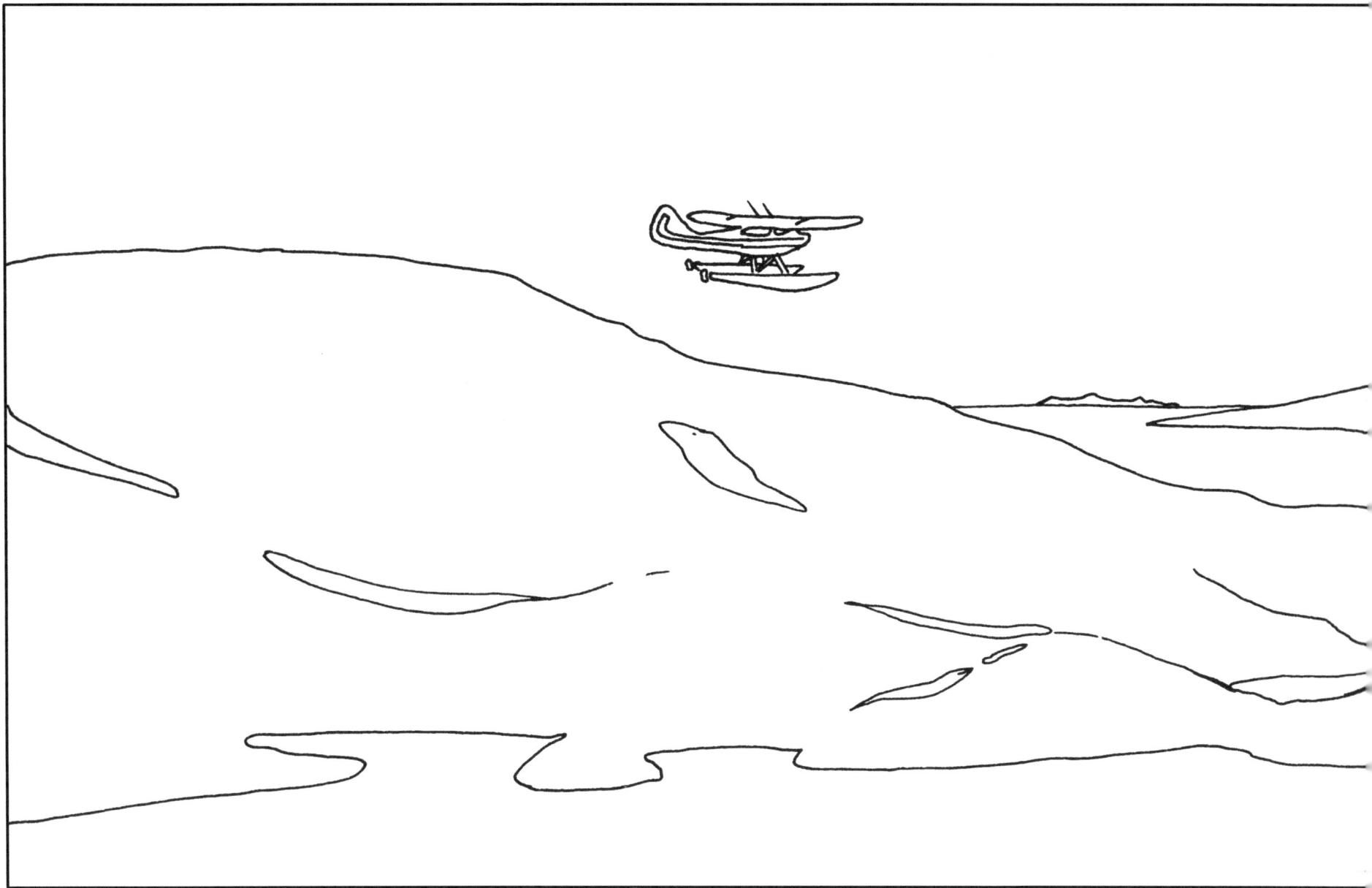

Hawkins Island   Peak Island   Point Gravina

A hike to Crater Lake or up Mt. Eyak will reveal a magnificent view of Orca Inlet and Prince William Sound. Crater Lake has some nice trout, so take your pole.

Sheep Point   Bomb Point   Knot Point   Salmo Point   Observation Island

Bear and deer have been seen on the mountain and in the fall there are many berries. On the Crater Lake trail, notice Kayak Island in the Gulf of Alaska far across the Copper River Flats.

Alaskan Brown Bear and Black Bear frequent the streams and meadows of Hartney Creek. They feed on the succulent green plants, spawning salmon and berries. Bears may be seen near any salmon spawning stream. View the tracks up close and the bears from a distance.

Spawning salmon can be easily seen during the late summer or fall in Hatchery Creek on Power Creek Road. They change color and shape as they prepare to spawn in the shallow gravel basins called redds. The eggs will hatch during the winter and in the spring, the smolts emerge.

Trumpeter Swans nest in the ponds of the Copper River Delta. This mother swan and her two signets share a pond on Long Island with a Common Merganser family. Though most migrate south, a couple dozen winter on Lake Eyak near the weir at Six Mile, Copper River Highway.

Mother Dusky Goose leads her goslings along the Sheridan River. The Copper River Delta is the only nesting area of the Dusky Canada Goose. Geese are common summer sights as the goslings, often in flocks of several dozen, are "babysat" while the parents forage for food.

Mountain Goats live high in the mountains. You can spot them on the mountains near Sheridan lacier and on Goat Mountain east of the Copper River using binoculars or a spotting scope. Look for small moving white spots against the dark grasses or rock.

This Bull Moose feeds near the Alaganik Picnic area. He'll loose his antlers in the fall and grow a whole new set next year. Moose, though huge, are hard to see because their color blends so well with the countryside. You have to stay still and watch or catch one moving to sight them.

Razor clams once made Cordova the "Clam Capital of the World." The earthquake of 1964 raised the beds too high for the clams and many beds were lost. Local residents know where to find some of the remaining beds. Clams were dug commercially on Kanak Island in the 1980s.

Silver fishing is a popular sport in August and September. Silvers can weigh almost twenty pounds and are great fighters. Try your luck at Fleming Spit, Eyak River, or Alaganik Slough. Cordova's annual silver salmon derby in August and September sends anglers in search of the largest fish.

Air Boats are used to travel the swamps and shallow sloughs of the delta. Their engines are very so you'll hear them even when they're far away. Airboats enable people to cover long distances away from the road quickly for sightseeing, fishing and hunting. A thrilling ride!

Three wheelers were popular transportation in 1986 and great fun. Many hunters use them to get to good hunting areas and to carry out the game. Others use them for picnicking, beach combing and riding around just for the fun of it. Four wheelers are commonly used in the 2020s.

Sheridan and Sherman Glaciers are visible from the Copper River Highway. A spur road takes you to Sheridan Glacier so you can walk right on the ice to see crevasses and caves or climb the moraine ridge to view bergs in the lake.

28

A raft trip across the Glacial Lake and down the Sheridan River was an exciting and fascinating way to spend a day. The ice bergs on the lake come in many fantastic and incredible shapes and the river offers thrilling rapids and a chance to see wildlife on the shore. In the 2020s, we can kayak among the icebergs on the ever-changing moraine lake.

Skaters enjoy the ice of Odiak Pond on a cold winter day. The frozen waterways are natural for hockey, countryside touring, and just plain old skating. After a period of rain, the ice can be unsafe to walk or skate on; it takes a long time of freezing weather to make the ice safe.

The Iceworm Festival is a highlight of the Cordova winter. Historic clues lead residents in the "Iceworm Tail Hunt" in the weeks prior to the parade. The Festival features contests, shows, and exhibits. The parade which features the 140-foot-long iceworm with his "found" tail.

Mount Eyak Ski Area has a lift which originally carried skiers in Sun Valley. On a clear day after a fresh winter snow, you'll find slopes to challenge expert skiers with a world-class view. Cross country skiing areas abound. Some of the Delta trails are spectacular on a moonlight night.

www.ingramcontent.com/pod-product-compliance
Lightning Source LLC
Chambersburg PA
CBHW050753090426

42737CB00004B/102